SHARP AND STICKY STUFF

ANIMAL WEAPONS

Lynn M. Stone

The Rourke Press, Inc.
Vero Beach, Florida 32964

PHOTO CREDITS
© Lynn M. Stone: cover, title page, p. 4, 8, 10, 13, 18, 21;
© Joe McDonald: p. 7, 12; © Breck P. Kent: p. 15;
© James P. Rowan: p. 17

Library of Congress Cataloging-in-Publication Data

Stone, Lynn M.
  Sharp and sticky stuff / Lynn M. Stone.
     p. cm. — (Animal Weapons)
  Includes index
  Summary: Describes a variety of weapons used by animals,
including stingers, quills, tongues, and webs.
  ISBN 1-57103-167-7
  1. Animal weapons—Juvenile literature.   [1. Animal weapons.]
I. Title II. Series. Stone, Lynn M. Animal weapons.
QL940.S745 1996
591.57—dc20   96–8997
                                                          CIP
                                                          AC

Printed in the USA

TABLE OF CONTENTS

SHARP AND STICKY STUFF

The animal world is full of danger. To survive, animals sometimes frighten, hurt, or kill each other.

For those actions some animals have **lethal** (LEE thul), or deadly, weapons. Many large animals have weapons that are easy to see, like teeth, claws, and horns.

Other animals, most of them quite small, have more unusual weapons. They can be such things as sticky nets, needles, spines, and dartlike tongues.

The spines of a cecropia moth caterpillar make it one of nature's pincushions

TONGUES

Most animal tongues are not weapons at all. Woodpeckers and anteaters, though, zap insects with their tongues. Toads flick out their tongues like darts to collect insects.

The chameleon's tongue works much like the toad's. The chameleon has a point-and-shoot tongue longer than its body. Its sticky tip grabs insects and even small birds and tiny mice!

The chameleon's sticky-tipped tongue picks off prey and returns it to the chameleon's waiting mouth

STINGERS

Bees and hornets generally use their stingers to keep other animals away from their homes.

A bee's sting doesn't stop a hungry honey bear, but it scares most animals away.

A bee stinger has **venom** (VEN um), or poison, on it. People who are **allergic** (uh LER jik) to bee venom can become seriously ill or even die.

The stinger is built like a tiny arrow with many arrowheads along it. Its shape makes it difficult to remove.

While it works to collect pollen, the bee's stinger is hidden. Bees use their stingers for defense

PORCUPINE QUILLS

Porcupine quills are long, hollow hairs. Each quill has a tiny hooked tip called a **barb** (BAHRB).

A porcupine is largely a plant eater, so it doesn't need to kill anything. The quills in its tail help it to defend itself against fishers, mountain lions, owls, and coyotes.

A porcupine delivers quills with a swat of its tail. The quills easily pull away from the porcupine and just as easily stick in the flesh of an enemy.

The porcupine doesn't throw quills. It delivers them with a swat of its tail

A woodpecker plunges its tongue into the crack of a tree for insects

The rhinoceros katydid of the Central American rain forest wears a sharp horn on its head and spurs on its legs

SPINES

Like porcupines, the little hedgehogs of Africa, Europe, and Asia are "pincushions."

Hedgehog spines aren't barbed, though. They don't pull loose and stick like arrows into an enemy.

Hedgehogs don't attack other animals. Their spines are for defense. Hedgehogs can roll into a ball covered by their own spines.

Many kinds of caterpillars are loaded with spines, too, as are lizards. Spines help these animals defend themselves from **predators** (PRED uh turz), the animals that might eat them.

The pygmy hedgehog depends upon spines to keep predators away

SPIDER WEAPONS

Spiders and their cousins, the scorpions, are fearsome hunters in their little worlds. They have a variety of weapons for catching and killing prey.

The scorpion has a lethal stinger that injects venom. The stinger of a large scorpion can kill small lizards.

Spiders have toothlike fangs that inject venom. The venom from scorpions and certain spiders can make people ill. Occasionally their venom kills someone.

The end of the death-stalker scorpion's body is a stinger that is lethal to small prey.

WEAPONS AND WEBS

Many spiders catch prey with "feet" near their mouths. These tiny grabbers hold prey until the spider can bite it.

A few kinds of spiders hang fancy webs. They're beautiful to us but lethal to insects. Sooner or later, insects crawl or fly into the sticky silk web.

The ogre-faced spider holds its web like a tiny net. When an insect steps near, the spider spreads the net over it.

This garden spider's silky web trapped a grasshopper

CHEMICAL WEAPONS

Certain animals have **chemical weapons** (KEM uh kul) (WEP unz) that their bodies make. Skunks, for example, fire a foul-smelling spray called **musk** (MUSK) to chase off enemies. Water snakes release musk, too.

Toads release a bitter, mildly poisonous liquid through their skin. Poison-arrow frogs have highly poisonous flesh. It's deadly to animals and people.

The spitting cobra can shoot a stream of venom into the eyes of an animal six feet away. The venom stings, and it can blind the cobra's enemy.

Bright colors of a poison-arrow frog's flesh is highly poisonous

SPURS AND NAILS

Ring-necked pheasants and other birds in their family wear lethal **spurs** (SPURZ) on their legs. A spur is a long, sharp claw. Males use the spurs as weapons in fights with each other.

The five-foot tall cassowary bird of Australia and New Guinea has a knifelike claw on the middle toe of each foot. The cassowary cannot fly, but the claw is a great defense. The bird's slashing kicks can easily kill a man.

Glossary

allergic (uh LER jik) — being highly sensitive in a harmful way to a drug, poison, or some other substance

barb (BAHRB) — a sharp point that juts backward from the main point, like an arrow or fishhook

chemical weapon (KEM uh kul) (WEP un) — liquid or gas substance made within an animal's body and used for defense or the taking of prey

lethal (LEE thul) — very dangerous; deadly

musk (MUSK) — an oily liquid with a foul smell

predators (PRED uh turz) — animals that hunt other animals for food

spurs (SPURZ) — long, sharp claws found on the legs of certain birds

venom (VEN um) — a poison produced by certain animals, including several snakes, fish, and spiders

INDEX